_____

Presented To

_____

Presented By

_____

Date

meditations & prayers
to bring you closer to God

PRAYER
Moments

inspirio

Prayer Moments
ISBN 0-310-80490-6

Copyright © 2004 by GRQ, Inc.
Brentwood, Tennessee 37027

Published by Inspirio™, The gift group of Zondervan
5300 Patterson Avenue, SE
Grand Rapids, Michigan 49530

Requests for information should be addressed to:
Inspirio™, The gift group of Zondervan
Grand Rapids, Michigan 49530
http://www.inspiriogifts.com

Editor: Lila Empson
Project Manager: Tom Dean
Manuscript written by Jan Dargatz
Design: Whisner Design Group, Tulsa, Oklahoma

Printed in China.

04 05 06 / 4 3 2 1

The earth is filled with your love, O LORD.

Psalm 119:64 *NIV*

Contents

Introduction 8

A Bigger God (Recognizing God's Power) 10

The Promotion (Recognizing God's Wisdom) 12

Two Thumbs Up (Thanksgiving) 14

Ten More Years (Boldly Asking) 16

Wanting to Want To (Developing Prayer Consistency) 20

Always the Best Answer (God's Answers) 22

Getting FAT (Personal Prayer) 24

Always Enough Time (Praying About Priorities) 26

An Even Better Answer (God's Perfect Answers) 30

The Dust Storm (Experiencing God's Presence) 32

The Walk Back (Prayer Story) 34

Protect Me Now (Praying for Protection) 38

Purified for Use (Praying for Purity) 40

Two Sacks Full (Praying for Provision) 44

No Distance in Prayer (Prayer Is Boundless) 46

Give Up Prescribing (Submitting to God) 48

God's Viewpoint (Praying for Enemies) 50

Plenty of Suds (Praying for Cleansing) 54

Only in Sales (Responsibility in Prayer) 56

Persisting with Patience (Persisting in Prayer) 58

SOS Signal (Emergency Prayers) 60

Clued In (God's Perfect Provision) 64

Knowing the Shepherd *(God Guides Us)* 66

The Cruise *(Prayer Story)* 68

Something Even Better *(Praying God's Best)* 72

A Safe Landing *(Praying for Safety)* 74

Knitting with God *(Experiencing His Presence)* 78

Seeing As God Sees *(Praying for Compassion)* 80

A Change of Heart *(Praying for Healing)* 82

Deeper Roots *(Praying for Others)*..84

Until You Cry *(Praying for Souls)* 88

The Job *(Praying for Favor)*..90

Go When You Know *(God Answers Prayer)* 92

Clearing the Way *(God Forgives)* 94

Used by God *(Prayer for Willingness)* 98

Remembering the Reason *(Praying with Intention)* 100

Divine Options *(Praying for Guidance)*..102

All Day Long *(Praying Without Ceasing)* 104

Without Getting Dizzy *(Yielding Control)* 108

Fear, Do Not Enter *(Prayer for Faith)* 110

The Shelter *(Prayer Story)* 112

Fret Thee Not *(Prayer Overcomes Anxiety)* 116

Become What You Pray *(Prayer Brings Change)* 118

Asking, Knocking, Seeking *(Importance of Prayer)* 122

Always the Right Time *(Praise and Thanksgiving)* 124

You are good, and what you do is good;
   teach me your decrees.
                              Psalm 119:68 NIV

Introduction

God is available 24/7. That very simple truth is at the core of the devotionals in this book.

Situations that warrant prayer can arise at any hour of any day. And God is available to hear prayers at any hour of the day or night—about anything—from anyone—in any situation or circumstance. There is no need for a person to use *thee* and *thou* language in talking to God. There is no subject that is off-limits for prayer. There is no need to be in a particular building or in a particular posture when praying. Prayer is simply having a conversation with God, and the good news is that he is always willing to talk.

Prayer Moments are slices of life that illustrate opportunities for talking to God. They are based upon modern-day, real people in real situations. The approach to prayer is rooted in Bible truth.

When you need a moment of inspiration and insight into prayer, these *Prayer Moments* devotionals are just right for you.

PRAYER
for Wisdom

Make our minds steadfast, strengthen us

against temptation, and keep us from all

unrighteousness. . . . Teach us to inwardly

love you before all things with a clean mind . . .

for you are our Maker and Redeemer. Amen.

King Alfred

*Yours, O LORD, is the greatness and the power
and the glory and the majesty and the splendor.*

1 Chronicles 29:11 NIV

A Bigger God

Libby was scrambling to get out of town on vacation and found herself staring at a mountain of paperwork on her desk. She sighed, "There's just n-o-o-o way."

"Is there anything more I can do to help you?" her secretary asked.

"No," sighed Libby. "These are all things I need to do personally."

Libby leaned back in her chair and closed her eyes. "Lord," she prayed. "I'm overwhelmed right now. This seems like a huge problem for me. But I believe you are bigger than any problem I might have—you certainly are bigger than this stack of paper on my desk. Please help me to see clearly what absolutely must be done before I leave town. Please help me to get things prepared so my staff can continue to work while I'm away."

*God is our refuge
and strength,
an ever-present
help in trouble.*

Psalm 46:1 NIV

Libby then dove into the work

before her. When she finished typing the last memo, correcting the last project report, and leaving the last message on an answering machine, she was shocked to see it was only eight o'clock.

"Thanks, Lord," she said aloud as she switched off the lights in her office.

A pause to pray can help you shift focus from a seemingly impossible task ahead to the eternal God who makes all things possible. Prayer can also help you approach a problem with renewed optimism and energy.

I am poor and needy; may the Lord think of me. You are my help and my deliverer; O my God, do not delay.

Psalm 40:17 NIV

Help me, God, to relax in your strength and to accomplish what you desire for me to do.
Amen.

You will keep in perfect peace
him whose mind is steadfast,
because he trusts in you.

Isaiah 26:3 NIV

The Promotion

Cliff's parents were in Europe. His two best friends were on a fishing trip. *Everybody I trust for wise counsel has left town this weekend*, Cliff said to himself as he dropped his briefcase on the entry-hall floor.

Cliff's boss had told him in a late-afternoon appointment that the company wanted him to transfer to another region. "Decide over the weekend," his supervisor had said. "If you go, there's a salary increase, the company will pay moving, and you'll be up for a promotion in six months."

"If I don't go?" Cliff had asked.

"Can't promise you any of that."

Commit to the LORD whatever you do, and your plans will succeed.

Proverbs 16:3 NIV

Cliff sat down in his easy chair and stared at the opposite wall. Deep inside the thought came, *The Lord is still in town.*

"What do you think, Lord?" Cliff prayed. "Should I stay or go?"

Immediately Cliff grabbed a legal pad and made two columns: YES/GO and NO/STAY. For the next two days, Cliff wrote down every pro and con that came to mind. On Sunday evening, he stared at what he had written and had his answer. "Thanks, Lord," he said, as he circled one set of words at the top of his lists.

Every major decision in life is an opportunity for God to reveal his wisdom to you and his will for you. Trust God to reveal his answers to yes-or-no questions and this-or-that choices.

You do not know what your life will be like tomorrow. . . . You ought to say, "If the Lord wills, we shall live and also do this or that."

James 4:14–15 NASB

Help me, God, to know what I should do. Let my choices and decisions please you.
Amen.

Two Thumbs Up

Hannah loved Saturday afternoons with her mother, Joan, and her Aunt Kay almost as much as they enjoyed being with six-year-old Hannah. Today's outing had been a trip to the zoo to see the recently completed penguin habitat. The afternoon had been punctuated by frequent photo opportunities and prolonged girl giggles.

It seemed appropriate that Saturday afternoon outings nearly always ended with pastries at the Tearoom of the Two Sisters. As their marzipan cakes were brought to the table this Saturday, Hannah quickly volunteered, "I'll pray."

"Of course," said Aunt Kay as she and Joan folded their hands and bowed their heads.

Joan and Kay had taught Hannah a number of simple childhood prayers, and they were eager to see which prayer Hannah chose to say in response to a day of penguins, loving hugs, giggles, marzipan cakes, and a tea party. Hannah, however, responded to them by saying boldly, "No, not like that."

Joan and Kay immediately opened their eyes and looked at Hannah. She beamed at them, gave a two-thumbs-up sign with her arms raised, smiled brightly as she looked heavenward, and said with exuberance, "Yea, God! Thanks."

Your expressions of thanksgiving to God do not need to be voiced in lofty words, long formal sentences, or with a hands-folded, eyes-closed posture. Your expressions of gratitude need only be intentional, a reflection of a heart brimming with enthusiasm for all God has provided.

Whatever you do in word or deed, do all in the name of the Lord Jesus, giving thanks through Him to God the Father.

Colossians 3:17 NASB

God, I am increasingly grateful to you, even for the little things that bring a smile to my heart this very hour.

Amen.

If we know that He hears us in whatever we ask, we know that we have the requests which we have asked from Him.

1 John 5:15 NASB

Ten More Years

Stanley was in bad health at the age of seventy. He related to a younger friend Ben, "I looked about me, and I saw so much spiritual opportunity left in the world and I felt I had a lot to give. I so yearned to continue that I went to God and said, 'Lord, give me ten more years, and let them be the most fruitful of my life.'"

Ben asked, "What did God say?"

"Stanley, you've got them."

Ben then asked, "How old are you now?"

"Seventy-eight," Stanley replied and added quickly, "I've got two more years."

Let us then approach the throne of grace with confidence, so that we may receive mercy.

Hebrews 4:16 NIV

Ben hesitated a moment but then ventured, "Well, what are you going to do then?"

With a twinkle in his eye Stanley said, "I'm going back for ten more years."

Ben later wrote to a friend: "I

think the reason we aren't bolder in prayer is because we think somehow it has already been decided. So the prayer that's heaviest on our heart, we don't pray. Everything I read in Scripture tells me God wants us to pray about our deepest desires. I've decided I'm going to pray for what I truly believe God wants me to have."

∽

God invites you to ask boldly for those things that even seem impossible—and then to trust him to answer your requests in his timing, by his methods, and according to his plan.

Jesus said, "If you remain in me and my words remain in you, ask whatever you wish, and it will be given you. This is to my Father's glory that you bear much fruit, showing yourselves to be my disciples."

John 15:7–8 NIV

Thank you, God, for the boldness to pray for the deepest yearning of my heart, and then to trust you to answer without error.

Amen.

PRAYER
God's Sovereign Will

May the strength of God pilot us.
May the power of God preserve us.
May the wisdom of God instruct us.
May the hand of God protect us.
May the way of God direct us.
May the shield of God defend us.
May the host of God guard us.
Against the snares of the evil ones,
Against the temptations of the world.

SAINT PATRICK

"Thy kingdom come. Thy will be done
in earth, as it is in heaven."

Matthew 6:10 KJV

PRAYER BRINGS [GOD] DOWN TO EARTH,
AND LINKS HIS POWER WITH OUR EFFORTS.

D. L. MOODY

I look up to the hills.
Where does my help come from?
My help comes from the LORD.
He is the Maker of heaven and earth.

Psalm 121:1–2 NIrV

Wanting to Want To

Georgia had been discussing prayer with her friend Meredith. "I believe I should pray more," Georgia said, "because I really do want to have a closer relationship with God, and I believe prayer is the way to develop that relationship. But it is very difficult for me to be consistent in praying."

Meredith suggested that Georgia try praying first thing in the morning or praying while she drove to work. "Those are great ideas," George responded. Then she admitted, "Prayer just seems hard to me. It's almost like dieting. I believe I should pray, just like I believe I should lose weight. But I just don't pray, just like I don't diet."

Every day I will praise you and extol your name for ever and ever.

Psalm 145:2 NIV

"I had that problem, too," Meredith said. "Do you know what I finally prayed?"

"What?" asked Georgia eagerly.

"I prayed, 'Lord, make me consistent in prayer.' And when that wasn't really my heart's desire, I prayed, 'Lord, make me want to be consistent in prayer.' And finally I prayed, 'Lord, make me want to want to be consistent in prayer.' I believe if you get to your true heart's desire, God will help you at that level."

∞

Prayer is a time for you to be totally honest with God. It is the time to tell God the deep desires of your heart and to tell God about your frustrations, needs, difficulties, and doubts—even if those frustrations and doubts are about prayer itself.

O LORD, hear my prayer, listen to my cry for mercy; in your faithfulness and righteousness come to my relief. Do not bring your servant into judgment, for no one living is righteous before you.
Psalm 143:1–2 NIV

Help me, God, to want to pray more and to have a deeper desire to spend time in your presence and in your word.
Amen.

Always the Best Answer

Jerry had been enjoying a day with his young nephew Zane—but then the begging started.

"Can you buy it for me? Please, please, please," Zane said while they were in the hardware store. A small, bright red pocket knife had caught Zane's attention.

"Someday I'll get you a pocket knife," Uncle Jerry replied. "But not today." Zane looked crestfallen, but Uncle Jerry knew his answer had been the right one for his nephew's safety.

"I'm hungry," Zane said an hour later. "Can I have some candy?"

Uncle Jerry was feeling a little hungry, too. "I have a better idea," he said. "Let's get a hamburger and a glass of milk, and then we can have ice cream later."

Later, Jerry reflected on the day with Zane. He thought, *God answers me in the same ways I answered Zane*

He guides the humble in what is right and teaches them his way.

Psalm 25:9 NIV

22

today. I may not like God's answers any more than Zane liked my answers, but I do believe that God loves me and wants what is good for me. Zane will understand my answers better some day, and perhaps someday I'll come to better understand some of God's answers to me.

∽

God hears and answers every prayer—but not always in the way you may want a prayer answered. His answers are yes, no, not now, yes if, and "something better."

"Because he loves me," says the LORD, "I will rescue him; I will protect him for he acknowledges my name. He will call upon me, and I will answer him."

Psalm 91:14–15 NIV

God, help me trust that the answer you give to my prayer is the best answer for me. *Amen.*

*This is the one to whom I will look,
to the humble and contrite in spirit.*

Isaiah 66:2 NRSV

Getting FAT

Margaret debated with herself all day about talking to her daughter, Elena. Early that morning, she had noticed Elena's Bible open on the dining table. In glancing down to see what she was reading, she saw a list titled "Prayer Needs" and under it the word FAT. Knowing that her daughter was about five pounds heavier now than when she went away to college, Margaret was concerned that Elena might be suffering from a poor self-image. She had mulled over all day what she might say. Finally she said simply, "I'm concerned, honey."

"What about?" Elena asked.

"I saw your prayer list," Margaret began hesitatingly. "I noticed the word *fat*. Honey, you said you'd only gained five pounds in four years. That's nothing. Now that you aren't eating dorm food—"

Blessed are they who keep his statutes and seek him with all their heart.

Psalm 119:2 NIV

Elena interrupted. "No, Mom. I'm

24

not praying about my weight. One of the college chaplains gave a talk and used FAT for the words Flexible, Agreeable, and Teachable. I'm praying I'll be flexible to do what God wants, agreeable in personality, and teachable as I read the Bible."

Greatly relieved, Margaret replied, "Well, in that case, I pray that I'll be FAT, too."

∽

God desires that you pray about character issues, including your perceived flaws, areas of weakness, and desires for personal growth. It's only when you recognize that you don't yet have the full character of Christ Jesus that you are truly humble in prayer.

I recounted my ways and you answered me; teach me your decrees. Let me understand the teaching of your precepts; then I will meditate on your wonders.

Psalm 119:26–27 NIV

My heart's desire, God, is to become the person that you want me to be—the person with whom you desire to live forever.

Amen.

*Evening, morning and noon
I cry out in distress,
and he hears my voice.*

Psalm 55:17 NIV

Always Enough Time

John felt as if he had been running all day. As he collapsed into bed, his mind was spinning. "Tomorrow will be a busy one, Lord," he said as he began to recount to God all he was anticipating the next day:

"The refinancing papers on the house need to be turned into the bank.

"Ben's college application has to be sent overnight if it's going to get there in time for scholarship consideration.

"The Wilson project is due at work, and I have five pages to write and two sets of data to analyze—"

Suddenly he stopped. "Lord, I seem to be putting too many things into my day—not just the day ahead of me, but most days. I'm starting to feel stressed out and uptight. Please help me to manage my time better. Show me, please, what you think is important, and help me not to try to fit into a twenty-four-hour day more than I can do."

*I say, "You are my
God." My times are
in your hands.*

Psalm 31:14–15 NIV

As John finished his prayer the thought came to him: *God made time. He certainly can show me how to use it.* John felt a weight lift from him and closed his eyes. He could sleep in peace.

Rather than ask God to expand your capacity or give more energy, there are times when you may be wiser to ask for God's help in adjusting priorities so your to-do list fits a normal working day.

He will be the sure foundation for your times, a rich store of salvation and wisdom and knowledge; the fear of the LORD is the key to this treasure.
Isaiah 33:6 NIV

Help me, God, to schedule my days wisely and to pursue the things that are most important in your eyes.
Amen.

PRAYER
A Blessed Nation

Almighty God: We make our earnest prayer that Thou wilt keep the United States in Thy holy protection: that Thou wilt incline the hearts of the citizens to cultivate a spirit of subordination and obedience to government, and entertain a brotherly affection and love for one another and for their fellow citizens of the United States at large.

GEORGE WASHINGTON

"If . . . My people who are called by My name humble themselves and pray and seek My face and turn from their wicked ways, then I will hear from heaven, will forgive their sin and will heal their land."

2 Chronicles 7:13–14 NASB

LET US PRAY THAT JESUS MAY REIGN OVER US
AND THAT OUR LAND MAY BE AT PEACE.

ORIGEN

*The LORD has looked down from heaven upon
the sons of men,
To see if there are any who understand,
Who seek after God.*

Psalm 14:2 NASB

*"As the heavens are higher than the earth,
So are My ways higher than your ways," says the LORD.*

Isaiah 55:9 NASB

An Even Better Answer

Randall had just moved to a new job in a new city. As he was unpacking a moving box in his new apartment, he prayed, "Lord, please give me some new friends in this new place."

As he prayed, Randall had in mind friends his own age. He hadn't counted on the Epperly, Peterson, or Jones children. There were nine children in his four-unit apartment building, ranging in age from three to twelve. By Randall's count, they had five bicycles, three basketballs, one baseball, and four baseball mitts—all of which seemed to be at his doorstep. Every day on returning home, he was greeted by the children: "Can you play with us? Can you read to me? Can you help me with my homework?"

This God—how perfect are his deeds, how dependable his words!

2 Samuel 22:31 GNT

On Randall's sixth-month anniversary in his apartment, the three families gave him a surprise party. The parents said, "You're the best thing that has happened to our children. They've never had an adult

30

friend like you. They look up to you and look forward to your arrival each evening after work. You have given each of them a real sense of purpose."

New friends? Yes, Randall thought, *they are some of my finest.*

In all circumstances, for everyone, and about everything, God has a plan and purpose. Prayer lines you up with what God has prepared for you. His ways are always superior to anything you—or any other person— could engineer.

This God is my strong refuge; he makes my pathway safe. He makes me sure-footed as a deer; he keep me safe on the mountains.
2 Samuel 22:33–34 GNT

I want to trust you more, God, to lead me into all that you desire for me to experience, learn, possess, enjoy, and do.
Amen.

In Your presence is fullness of joy;
In Your right hand there are pleasures forever.

Psalm 16:11 NASB

The Dust Storm

From the time Fred was a boy, he loved trucks. No one in his family was surprised that he became a truck driver. For Fred's part, he was grateful that most of his trips were short hauls so he could be close to his family and friends.

As much as Fred loved trucks, he hated dust storms. He had been stuck in one when he was a boy. He was convinced that it was only the kindness of a passing truck driver that had spared his family suffocation by the smothering dust that stalled their car.

Now, Fred found himself caught in a fierce dust storm that had blown into the desert. Panic was welling up in him: "Lord, help me. You know I hate this. I can hardly see to keep this rig on the road." To help him concentrate, Fred flicked off the radio talk show he had been listening to. But the last words of the broadcast stuck in his mind, "I'm here to tell you . . ."

I call to the LORD, who is worthy of praise, and I am saved from my enemies.

2 Samuel 22:4 NIV

Fred felt a comforting balm move through his soul and fill the cab. "You're not only here to tell me, Lord. You're here with me," Fred prayed. "Thank you."

God hears your SOS prayers. He responds with his power and wisdom to the circumstances that create emergencies in your life. He also responds to your heart's cry with his comforting presence.

In my distress I called to the LORD; I called out to my God. From his temple he heard my voice; my cry came to his ears.

2 Samuel 22:7 NIV

Be with me, God, in this moment, this day, this time, this season.
Amen.

The Walk Back

Jenna and Tamara had been in England for a month when they decided to venture out one evening to attend a special lecture Jenna saw advertised at the university where she was studying. Tamara had already graduated from college and had joined her friend for an adventure abroad. She felt fortunate to be working in a temp position but had been eager to experience a bit of her friend's university life.

The two young women had taken a bus from the youth hostel where they were living to a lecture hall several blocks from the campus, and they now found themselves back at the bus stop, feeling mentally enriched by the new ideas they had heard and feeling full from several cookies and three cups of tea.

They had watched groups of people leave the lecture hall in cars, and soon the parking lot was empty. A man, apparently the caretaker of the building, finally exited the lecture hall and locked the door behind him.

"Your transport hasn't come yet?" he asked.

"We're waiting for the bus," Jenna replied.

"Past time," the man said as he pulled a watch from his

pocket. "The busses don't run after 10:30 on weeknights."

"But how will we get home?" Jenna asked.

The man peered into the darkness of the empty parking lot. "I don't know, lass," he said. "I could call for a taxi, but there's no phone in the hall. Looks like you'll have to walk."

"How are you getting home?" Tamara interjected.

"Oh, I live just two doors down. I'd help you, but I don't have a car and I don't have a phone." And with that, the man shuffled quickly into the darkness before the girls could ask another question.

"Thank you, anyway, for offering . . ." Tamara said, her voice trailing off.

"We'd better start," replied Jenna. "We've wasted precious time. It's not only dark and late, but the fog is rolling in fast."

"Which way?" Tamara asked.

"That way," Jenna said, pointing to what she hoped was south. "I think.

After three blocks of walking in silence, the two young women paused under the streetlight at an intersection. "Anything familiar?" Tamara asked.

"No," said Jenna. "I can't believe we waited twenty minutes for a bus that wasn't coming."

Tamara said softly, "We're in trouble."

"I think we need to pray," said Jenna.

"I agree," said Tamara.

"Lord," Jenna began, "we don't have the foggiest idea where we are . . ." Suddenly aware of Tamara's little laugh at what she had unintentionally said, she added, ". . . in this thick fog. All we know is that we're lost and it's dark and there's nobody around. You know where we are. You know the way."

"We trust you to get us home safely," Tamara added. "Please protect us."

The fog eventually grew so thick the two young women could not see more than ten feet ahead. Nevertheless, at each intersection, under the eerie light of a fog-shrouded streetlight, they paused to pray, "Straight ahead or make a turn, Lord?" Each time they felt they should continue on without turning. Then Jenna said after a prayer, "I think we need to turn now."

"Whatever you say," said Tamara.

Two blocks later, they found themselves staring into the blackness of what appeared to be a park. "It's the commons," Jenna said. "I know where we are."

Within ten minutes they were at the hostel. They opened the door quickly and were amazed at the time on the lobby clock. The weeknight curfew for the all-female hostel was midnight. On this night, the clock in the lobby read 11:58.

"Thank you, thank you, thank you, Lord," Jenna prayed as they climbed the stairs to their room. "Me too, me too, me too," Tamara added.

Once they had made a pot of tea to warm themselves, Tamara reflected. "I know we were lost, but we made only two turns, and they were the correct ones. We really didn't waste any steps."

"You're right," said Jenna with a sigh. "I'm just so grateful to be warm and safe. Next time we'll know better."

"The good thing," reflected Tamara, "is that the Lord did know better. He knew exactly what was happening. The Lord knew the bus schedule, and he allowed this to happen for some reason."

"Maybe to teach us to trust him more," said Jenna.

All that Jenna and Tamara concluded that night was underscored even more when they awoke the next day and heard the morning news. Two convicted rapists had been taken into police custody a little before midnight—they had been arrested just two blocks south of where Jenna and Tamara had made their turn. As the girls retraced their steps on a map, they realized they had taken the last turn they could have taken before the road divided. Had they gone just one more block south without turning, they would have been separated from the commons by a water inlet.

"Thank you, Lord," Tamara prayed after they heard the news. "Me too," Jenna added softly, tears silently flowing down her cheeks.

LORD, teach me your ways. Lead me along a straight path.

Psalm 27:11 NIrV

O LORD, *be not far off;*
O You my help, hasten to my assistance.

Psalm 22:19 NASB

Protect Me Now

Christina rarely missed her early-morning, thirty-minute jog through her neighborhood. There were several routes she enjoyed, each of which had its own beauty. She enjoyed the time alone, the fresh air, and the awareness of the changing seasons. She often made her jog a time of prayer or recited Scriptures she was memorizing. When she thought about the experience later, she concluded that her concentration on spiritual matters had probably kept her from noticing that the Parkers' gate was standing wide open. Had she noticed, she would have changed her route immediately. The Parkers' large, black dog was not something she wanted to encounter on an open road. She had been bitten once by a large, black dog and was not eager for a repeat experience.

You give me your shield of victory; you stoop down to make me great.

2 Samuel 22:36 NIV

But there he was. Running toward her. Fast. Christina quickened her pace but then realized there was no way she could outrun the dog. She stopped, crouched down, and

38

prepared to be attacked, praying as she did, "Lord, help me. Help me now."

To her amazement, the dog did not attack. It stopped barking, came closer as if to investigate her strange behavior, then leaned forward and licked her cheek.

∞

Throughout the Bible, men and women cried out to God in times of distress and grave danger—for rescue, security, preservation, and deliverance. You, too, can trust God to hear your prayers.

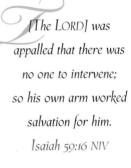

[The LORD] was appalled that there was no one to intervene; so his own arm worked salvation for him.

Isaiah 59:16 NIV

God, please protect me. Shield me from attacks that might come against me. Uphold me in your everlasting arms. *Amen.*

He will sit as a refiner and purifier of silver; he
will purify . . . and refine them like gold and silver.

Purified for Use

Jeanette did not recall ever seeing anything man-made that was quite so captivating in its beauty. She had just completed a ninety-minute tour of a South African gold mine. The tour had followed all the stages of the mining and refining process beginning with the locating of a strain of ore deep in the mine. In the final stage, a cascading stream of molten, purified gold was poured into molds. The gold shimmered in the sunlight, the metal nearly transparent in the intense heat.

The guide allowed the tourists to stand in silent awe for a few moments, and then taking a bar of cool, purified gold, she showed how soft it was—malleable to the touch, easily molded and shaped.

"O Lord," Jeannette found herself praying, "purify me. Let me see that the difficult experiences of my life are part of your refining process intended to burn away the impurities from my heart. Help me to understand that what may

Set an example . . . in speech, in life, in love, in faith and in purity.

1 Timothy 4:12 NIV

seem like impossibily hard circum-
sances can be used by you to make
me the person you desire me to be.
Radiate your beauty in me. Mold me
and make me—fashion and shape
me—into the person you want me
to be."

_God uses prayer to refine your
character—to burn away impurities
of hatred, anger, resentment and bit-
terness, guilt, and sin—and to replace
those impurities with the beauty of
holiness, faith, joy, peace, and love._

_Draw near to God and
He will draw near to
you. Cleanse your
hands, you sinners; and
purify your hearts, you
double-minded. . . .
Humble yourselves in
the presence of the
Lord, and He will
exalt you._
James 4:8, 10 NASB

God, I trust you to refine
me into something that
you see as pure.
Amen.

PRAYER
for Freedom

*Almighty God, you have made us for
yourself, and our hearts are restless till
they find rest in you. Grant us purity of
heart and strength of purpose, that no
selfish passion may hinder us from
knowing your will, and no weakness
hinder us from doing it; but that in your
light we may see light, and in your
service find our perfect freedom;
through Jesus Christ our Lord.*

SAINT AUGUSTINE
OF HIPPO

Jesus said, "If the Son sets you free, you will be free indeed."

❦

John 8:36 NIV

REAL FREEDOM IS NOT FREEDOM FROM, BUT FREEDOM FOR.

ROBERT W. YOUNG

It is for freedom that Christ has set us free. Stand firm, then, and do not let yourselves be burdened again by a yoke of slavery.

❦

Galatians 5:1 NIV

Two Sacks Full

Pauline stared into the cupboard and wondered how she was going to feed herself and her three children nourishing meals. A cutback at the factory meant fewer hours for both Pauline and her husband, and the decrease in family income threatened her ability to maintain their home and keep food on the table. Her husband had taken a part-time job in a neighboring town, but they wouldn't see any income from that job for several more days.

A verse from Sunday's service came to her mind: "Every animal of the forest is mine, / and the cattle on a thousand hills" (Psalm 50:10 NIV). "When you have a need," the pastor had preached, "ask God to butcher one of his cattle for you." Pauline did just that, and then she bundled up her children to take them to midweek Bible study.

That evening as they returned home, the children raced to the porch,

*He upholds the
cause of the
oppressed and
gives food to
the hungry.*

Psalm 146:7 NIV

where they spied two grocery sacks. "Look, Mom. Someone went shopping for us," Becky said.

The sacks were filled with canned goods, dried beans, flour, and two packets of ground beef. Pauline smiled. Thank you, God.

Throughout the Bible, whenever God's people—those who worshiped and obeyed him—looked to God to provide the basics of life for them, he never disappointed them. He always supplied the food, water, and shelter they needed.

Then the word of the LORD came to Elijah: . . . "You will drink from the brook, and I have ordered the ravens to feed you there."
1 Kings 17:2, 4 NIV

God, you see all my circumstances. Help me to trust you to provide all that my loved ones and I need.
Amen.

*Trust in the LORD with all your heart
and lean not on your own understanding . . .
and he will make your paths straight.*

Proverbs 3:5–6 NIV

No Distance in Prayer

Helene, a young missionary in Indonesia, felt discouraged and sad as she sat in the Jakarta airport. Leaving her terminally ill mother had been particularly tough. She loved her work in the missionary school and felt called by God to return to Indonesia, but her heart was heavy nonetheless.

As she waited for the small plane that would take her to one of the other islands, she found herself gazing at the row of clocks in the airport. One told the time in Riyadh, Saudi Arabia, another the time in Sydney, Australia, still another the time in London, England. Her eyes landed on the clock that gave the time in New York City, and she suddenly realized that back home, it was Sunday morning, and church was just about to

*He will not let your
foot slip—he who
watches over you will
not slumber.*

Psalm 121:3 NIV

begin. She reflected on the previous Sunday's service and the pastor's prayer for her. He had promised her before the entire congregation that they would be praying for her as part of the service every Sunday until she returned.

"There's no distance in prayer," Helene said quietly, her heart filling with renewed confidence and comfort. "What they are praying there, I will live out here."

Prayer has no boundaries. God—who sees you when you're praying and when you are being prayed about—answers out of his righteousness and compassion, regardless of your circumstances or distances.

May the LORD watch between you and me when we are absent one from the other.
Genesis 31:49 NASB

Help me to trust you, God, to see every detail of my need. You are neither farsighted nor shortsighted.
Amen.

Give Up Prescribing

The flower beds seemed to get larger by the hour. Kim had purchased several dozen bulbs to plant in the yard of her new home. She knew the time was running out to get them into the ground—this cool, sunny Saturday might be her last good day since a freeze was predicted early the following week. The harder she worked, however, the more bulbs she seemed to have to plant.

"I wonder when these will come up and bloom?" she asked aloud, with no one in earshot. "And I wonder what color these flowers will be—or even what kind of flowers they'll be." The bundles of bulbs had been labeled "assorted spring bulbs." She recognized tulip and hyacinth bulbs. A few others had been mysteries.

The longer Kim planted, the more she reflected. *So many things in my life are like these bulbs,* she thought.

I really don't know what God will provide in answer to my prayers— not exactly—or when he will provide the answers. Then she concluded, *But I know his gifts are good. After all, he's never made an ugly flower.*

God often provides an answer to your prayers—a provision for a need, an answer for a doubt, a solution for a problem—that you cannot antici- pate by human reason. God seems to delight in doing the mysterious, the miraculous, and the sublime.

The secret things belong to the LORD our God but the things revealed belong to us and to our sons forever, that we may observe all the words of this law.

Deuteronomy 29:29 NASB

When I can't see or know what's coming, God, help me to trust that you see all things and understand all mysteries.
Amen.

God's Viewpoint

Larry had enjoyed his job for years, but in the last six months, since Eugene had been his new supervisor, he found it increasingly difficult to go to work with a good attitude.

Larry could point to numerous things he didn't like about Eugene, including his critical attitude, micromanagement style, generally pessimistic attitude, and lack of creative flair. Still, Eugene was the boss, and Larry had a duty to follow his lead.

One morning when Larry was feeling particularly upset with Eugene, he found himself praying, "God, help me. I just can't take this anymore." He then opened his desk to take out a notepad, and his eyes fell upon an inspirational calendar he kept there. The inspirational thought for the day read, "Pray for those who irritate you." Larry sighed and said quietly, "Well, God, that was pretty direct."

Do everything in love.

1 Corinthians 16:14 NIV

Larry began to pray for Eugene every morning. He prayed about specific projects at work, specific personality attributes in Eugene, and for needs he knew Eugene was facing. Larry saw no overnight changes in Eugene, but that didn't mean nothing was changing. What Larry soon realized was that his own heart was changing.

⌇

Prayer gives you greater empathy for another person, and very often it changes your perspective. That change in perspective can produce a change in behavior that can in turn produce a change in a relationship.

Live in harmony with one another; be sympathetic, love as brothers, be compassionate and humble. Do not repay evil with evil or insult with insult, but with blessing, because to this you were called so that you may inherit a blessing.
1 Peter 3:8–9 NIV

God, I pray today for your best in the lives of those who irritate me. Help me to respond to them with patience and a smile.
Amen.

PRAYER
a Thankful Heart

*A*lmighty and gracious Father, we give you
thanks for the fruits of the earth in their
season and for the labors of those who harvest
them. Make us, we pray, faithful stewards of
your great bounty, for the provision of our
necessities and the relief of all who are in
need, to the glory of your Name,
through Jesus Christ our Lord, who
lives and reigns with you and the
Holy Spirit, one God, now and
for ever. Amen.

THE BOOK OF
COMMON PRAYER

Sing and make music in your heart to the Lord. Always give thanks to God the Father for everything. Give thanks to him in the name of our Lord Jesus Christ.

Ephesians 5:19–20 NIrV

GOD HAS TWO DWELLINGS: ONE IN HEAVEN, AND
THE OTHER IN A MEEK AND THANKFUL HEART.

Izaak Walton

*Give thanks to the LORD, because he is good.
His faithful love continues forever.*

Psalm 106:1 NIrV

If we confess our sins, he is faithful and just and will forgive us our sins.

1 John 1:9 NIV

Plenty of Suds

Jake stood under the pulsating massage showerhead and felt himself relaxing as the hot water poured over his freshly scrubbed body. He had just returned from a week of camping with friends in the high-mountain meadows several hours away. The water was soothing not only to his body but also to his soul.

Jake had come home feeling unsatisfied. The scenery had been beautiful as always. The fresh air and crisp nights had been a welcome relief from the summer heat in the valley. But the conversations he and his friends had shared had left him feeling uneasy. He had listened to stories he wished he hadn't heard, laughed at jokes that he hadn't really found funny, and partaken of some substances he wished he hadn't touched.

Cleanse me with hyssop, and I will be clean, wash me, and I will be whiter than snow.

Psalm 51:7 NIV

"God, I feel dirty on the inside as well as the outside," Jake prayed. "Please cleanse me. Please forgive me."

54

As the dirty, sudsy water swirled into the drain at his feet, Jake felt as if the guilt in his heart was also being washed away. "There's nothing like being clean—really clean," he said as he reached for a towel.

One of the most important prayers you can pray is an admission of a need for forgiveness from God and a request for an inner cleansing of the soul—a washing away of sins and all negative emotions, thoughts, and memories.

"Come now, let us reason together," says the LORD. "Though your sins are like scarlet, they shall be as white as snow."
Isaiah 1:18 NIV

God, please forgive me today and wash away all feelings of guilt and shame from my heart. Amen.

The one who calls you is faithful and he will do it.

1 Thessalonians 5:24 NIV

Only in Sales

Josh had just finished the first three weeks of his summer internship at a company about a hundred miles away from his home. He had enjoyed every minute of his first year of business studies, and he had looked forward to an opportunity to get some practical experience in the sales and marketing division of a firm out in the real world.

In a call to his father, a corporate executive, Josh described his experiences on the sales route he had been assigned, and he concluded, "I thought I'd see more results, Dad. The buyers just don't seem to respond to my sales pitch in the way I hoped. I'm a little discouraged."

May our Lord Jesus Christ . . . encourage your hearts and strengthen you in every good deed and word.

2 Thessalonians 2:16–17 NIV

His father replied, "Josh, never forget to pray for the potential buyer. Explain your product's benefits the best you can. Then leave the consequences up to God. He's management—you're only in sales."

Josh hung up the phone with a great sense of relief and a renewed enthusiasm for the weeks ahead. His father's words gave him a good game plan—pray first, work to the best of your ability, and leave the consequences up to God.

No matter the profession, you do well to pray about your work, do your best, and leave the management of results up to God. God alone knows all the methods available and the right time and ways for you to use those methods to produce results.

God is not unjust; he will not forget your work and the love you have shown him as you have helped his people and continue to help them.
Hebrews 6:10 NIV

God, please help me treat other people well, speak the truth, and work to the best of my ability. I trust you with the consequences.
Amen.

Let us not become weary in doing good, for at the proper time we will reap a harvest if we do not give up.

Galatians 6:9 NIV

Persisting with Patience

Charlotte was eagerly looking forward to her first face-to-face visit with Elisa in five years. Elisa was the daughter of a couple she and her husband had met forty years before. The families had stayed in touch after Charlotte and her husband had moved, and to Charlotte's delight, Elisa had attended college in the town where they had relocated. She had enjoyed having Elisa over to their home for tea and weekend visits, not only during college but also in the years that followed. In many ways, Elisa became the daughter Charlotte never had.

Through the years, Charlotte had talked to Elisa a great deal about God. She had been quick to pray with Elisa about problems Elisa faced. Mostly, however, Charlotte had prayed in secret, asking God to speak to Elisa's heart in ways only he could. At times she felt discouraged, wondering if her thirty years of prayer had meant anything. But on this day, she felt great excite-

Be strong and take heart, all you who hope in the LORD.

Psalm 31:24 NIV

ment in her heart at seeing Elisa. She had renewed hope.

"Help me to trust you, Lord," Charlotte prayed. "All things are in your timing. Help me to remain both persistent in prayer and patient."

You can't change another person's heart or will, even with persistent prayer. Only God can change a heart. Your role is to persist in prayer, trusting God to do his work in his timing.

Neither he who plants nor he who waters is anything, but only God, who makes things grow.

1 Corinthians 3:7 NIV

God, help me to do my part—to persist patiently in prayer. Help me to trust you to do what only you can do.
Amen.

Hear my prayer, O LORD;
let my cry come to you.

Psalm 102:1 NRSV

SOS Signal

Four men who attended the same church were discussing the pastor's sermon on prayer as they enjoyed their early morning coffee in the local café. Their discussion turned to the times when they believed their personal prayers were the strongest and most effective.

"I'm with the pastor," farmer Jim said. "I do my best praying when I'm driving my truck out to the fields as the sun comes up."

Frank, a hardware salesman, said, "I like to pray at night. That way I can tell God all about the problems of the day and thank him for all the good things that have happened."

O LORD. . . .Be our strength every morning, our salvation in time of distress.

Isaiah 33:2 NIV

Rod, a newspaperman, added his experience. "The most effective time for me to pray is when I'm alone with God in my fishing boat at the lake."

Earl, a telephone lineman, then voiced his opinion. "I know I should pray more in the quiet times of my life, but I'll tell you this—the best, boldest, and most effective praying I have ever done is when I find myself dangling upside down from a telephone pole." He smiled. "That's when I seem to be inspired."

Any time is a good time to pray. God does not only hear your prayers voiced in quiet reflection and sincerity, but also your SOS prayers in times of urgent emergency.

O God . . . give ear to me and hear my prayer. Show the wonder of your great love, you who save by your right hand those who take refuge in you from their foes.

Psalm 17:6–7 NIV

God, thank you for hearing my prayers at any time and every time, no matter the circumstance. Thank you for always being there. *Amen.*

PRAYER

Spiritual Preparation

Have Thine own way, Lord!

Have Thine own way!

Thou art the potter.

I am the clay.

Mold me and make me after Thy will,

While I am waiting, yielded and still.

ADELAIDE A. POLLARD

*"I alone know the plans I have for you, plans to
bring you prosperity and not disaster, plans
to bring about the future you hope for," says the LORD.*

Jeremiah 29:11 GNT

LORD, PREPARE ME FOR WHAT YOU ARE
PREPARING FOR ME.

CORRIE TEN BOOM

*"Don't I have the right to do with you people of Israel
what the potter did with the clay? You are in my hands
just like clay in the potter's hands," said the LORD.*

Jeremiah 18:6 GNT

Jesus said, "Your Father knows what you need before you ask him."

Matthew 6:8 NRSV

Clued In

When Rachel and Paul first left for an overseas business assignment, they thought they'd be away for three months. Fourteen years later, they found themselves settling into their fifth international home. Having lived in Asia, Europe, Australia, and now the Middle East, Rachel felt like an expert among the other corporate wives, who were struggling to find their way. She said to a group of them in a welcome-to-the-neighborhood meeting, "I've been where you are. I know what it means to suddenly feel totally unsure about things I used to do routinely, such as make a phone call, buy vegetables in the market, pay an electric bill, or talk to a cab driver."

Guide me in your truth and teach me, for you are God my Savior.

Psalm 25:5 NIV

Rachel then shared what she called her most practical advice: "Stay tuned in to God, who is totally clued in to all things. He knows how to do everything that you don't know how to do in this new nation. He knows where you need to go, whom you need to contact, and what words you need to say. There's nothing you need that God doesn't already know. I frequently say to God, 'I don't have a clue. You do. Lead me step by step.' And he does."

Only God is omniscient and omnipresent—all knowing and present at all times and in all places. When you turn to God in prayer, you are in essence asking God to give you precise and timely information and understanding out of his infinite and eternal storehouse of wisdom.

I thank and praise you, O God of my fathers: You have given me wisdom and power, you have made known to me what we asked of you.
Daniel 2:23 NIV

God, I don't have a clue what to do, how to do it, or what to say. Please give me your answers and directives.
Amen.

My help comes from the LORD,
the Maker of heaven and earth.

Psalm 121:2 NIV

Knowing the Shepherd

Wilma, at age eighty-eight, was considered the senior member of the women's service club in her community. One day a young woman in her thirties asked her, "Wilma, what's your secret? You always seem so calm and yet enthusiastic about the future, even when the world seems to be crumbling like a cookie. Nothing seems to upset you."

Wilma smiled and said, "I have a little prayer I've been praying every day for more than a half centruy. I pray it every morning when I first get up, and it starts my day off right. It goes like this: 'I'm just a little lamb, and you, God, are the shepherd. I don't know where to find everything I need. You'll have to show me. I can't make sense of a lot that goes on. You'll have to teach me what I need to know. I can't defend myself very well. You'll have to protect me. I'm prone to getting lost and to stumbling into places I shouldn't go. You'll have to lead me. I'm pretty much totally helpless, God.

The LORD is my shepherd, I shall not be in want.

Psalm 23:1 NIV

But I believe that you are a good shepherd and that you'll take care of your little lamb Wilma."

Wilma then smiled at the young woman and added, "And every day, he does."

God truly is the good shepherd for everyone who is willing to be part of his flock. He leads you and guides you in ways that only he knows, to destinations that are always for your eternal good.

I am always with you; you hold me by my right hand. You guide me with your counsel, and afterward you will take me into glory.
Psalm 73:23–24 NIV

God, I need your help. Thank you in advance for being there every second of every minute of every hour of my day.
Amen.

The Cruise

How wonderful are the good things you keep for those who honor you! Everyone knows how good you are, how securely you protect those who trust you.

Psalm 31:19 GNT

Marcy wasn't expecting "The Love Boat," but she was hoping for a little romance. From the minute she read the brochure about the Christian cruise, she had been daydreaming about sun, fun, and perhaps a new male friend with whom to enjoy the shore excursions that sounded exotic enough to be interesting and tame enough to be safe.

"Could this be for me?" she asked God as she read through the details of the five-days-at-sea adventure. She interpreted her little-faster heartbeat and unending interest in the trip as a yes. Within days she had sent her deposit. Now, two months later, she was standing on the deck of the luxury liner staring down at the dock. Her bags were unpacked, and she had changed into sandals and a sundress. She felt ready to cruise.

Marcy's husband, a firefighter, had been killed in the line of duty five years before. He had been her high school sweetheart, the love of her life. For four years after his death, she had felt mostly numb, fairly certain she would never love again. Her days had been fully occupied getting her twins, Ted and Tess, through high school.

68

Last fall Ted and Tess had left for college a hundred miles away, and Marcy found herself on a number of occasions walking aimlessly around the house. She had once again faced waves of grief and, realizing she had not dealt with some of the troubling doubts lingering in her soul, she had asked her friend and prayer partner, Ellie, to help her confront her questions—"Why Sam?" "Why then?" "Why me?" "What now?"

At last Marcy had come to the end of her questions, and she had felt tremendous relief as she had prayed, "Lord, I fully place Sam in your everlasting care. Thank you for letting me love him, and for preparing him to be my husband and the father of our twins. Help me to be open, now, to what you have for me in this next season of my life. If you so desire, send me someone to love."

Marcy was very specific about the kind of man she desired. He had to be a Christian, honest, hard-working, kind, and communicative. "Please, God," she had prayed, "give him a great sense of humor. And please let him be taller than I am." Since Marcy was five feet ten inches tall, she felt that last bit of prayer important to voice.

Three days into the cruise, Marcy was a little discouraged. She had concluded within twenty-four hours that the man of her dreams was not on board. Most of the passengers were the age of her parents—lovely people, but elderly. She had met the cruise social director, who had casually said to Marcy, "I'm surprised you chose this cruise. The younger set usually goes on the cruise two weeks from now."

Marcy was puzzled. Had she misread the brochure? Had she overlooked that rather important detail? She prayed, "God, I give this all to you." She determined to have a good time anyway.

And she did. Marcy made friends with one couple especially. Bill and Ruth were full of fun and always seemed to be wearing yellow, Marcy's favorite color. They had met for dinner every evening and had gone on two shore excursions together. Marcy had seen family photographs and had heard the story of how they had met forty-seven years ago.

It seemed entirely natural that Bill and Ruth would invite Marcy to their home in the mountains and that she would accept. Marcy suspected they would be lifelong friends.

Two days later, it was time to leave the ship. The week hadn't been what Marcy had anticipated, but she nonetheless felt rested and was significantly more tan. She had thoroughly enjoyed Christian concerts, had made some beautiful purchases, had enjoyed exquisite meals, and had been to the spa twice. Most of all, she had made friends who seemed more like family. In her prayers the last night of the cruise, Marcy had prayed sincerely, "Thank you, Lord, for letting me meet Bill and Ruth. I know their friendship is a gift from you."

"You look fabulous," Ruth said the final morning as she came to give Marcy a hug as they all waited to disembark. Bill added with a twinkle in his eye, "We're counting the days 'til you come to our mountain home. I promise you a good grilled steak."

Marcy nodded and replied cheerfully, "Can't wait. I have July eight to fifteen marked on my calendar."

"What? Is there a party?" a booming voice said behind Marcy. Ruth exclaimed, "Greg, how were you able to get on board? How wonderful. You can help us with our bags."

"That's why I'm here," Greg added with a big laugh. "Your number-one son is reporting for duty."

Bill said, "Marcy, meet our son Greg."

Marcy stammered. "Your son?"

"I thought I told you about Greg," said Ruth. "He's been on an overseas business assignment the last few years since his wife was killed in a car accident."

"They didn't tell you about me?" Greg said with his father's twinkle in his eye. "Well, I'll tell you. It sounds as if we're going to be at my folks house at the same time in July."

Greg was taller than Marcy's five-ten. She smiled.

He will teach us what he wants us to do; we will walk in the paths he has chosen.
Isaiah 2:3 GNT

To him who is able to do immeasurably more than all we ask or imagine . . . to him be glory.

Ephesians 3:20–21 NIV

Something Even Better

Tim had been car shopping for several weeks. He had weighed buying a new car versus a used car, a small car versus a midsize car, a truck versus a station wagon. Mostly, however, Tim was determined not to go over his budget. One day his friend Todd said, "You are always talking about what you can afford. I'd like to hear your answer to this question: What is it that you think God would like for you to drive?"

Tim responded candidly, "I don't think I ever gave that a thought. Maybe I'd better ask." Tim prayed for several days about the car God might like him to have. When Todd called later in the week, Tim said, "The more I prayed about this, the more I realized God always does things the best way. I was looking for the best deal, not necessarily the best car for me and my family. As I prayed, I realized that I hadn't considered how we anticipate our needs to change in the next year or so. Thank God I've got that figured out now. Praying about this made me

God had planned something better for us.

Hebrews 11:40 NIV

72

see that I'm going to have to save my money for eight more months, and I'm not sure of the exact make and model. But I know this: I'll have used wisely the resources God gave me, and he will help me to find the best car."

Prayer helps you to evaluate your choices and decisions from God's higher and better perspective. Prayer helps you recognize that God often desires for you to accomplish more or to seek greater excellence—not for his benefit but for your reward.

This is my prayer: that your love may abound more and more in knowledge and depth of insight, so that you may be able to discern what is best.
Philippians 1:9–10 NIV

God, I want your very best. Help to understand what that is, and then to pursue your highest and most excellent plan for my life.
Amen.

From the depths . . . I called for help,
and you listened to my cry.

Jonah 2:2 NIV

A Safe Landing

Ken had never skied, but when friends invited him
to join them on a trip to the Colorado mountains, he
eagerly accepted. His friends, knowing he was a novice,
had taken him shopping for the gear they called essen-
tial. Ken had followed them gladly from store to store.
The bus was chartered, the rooms reserved, the lift
passes purchased. Ken felt he was just along for the
ride. And that, he later concluded, was the way he
found himself at the top of a slope that seemed more
like a sheer cliff.

What could he do? "I don't have a prayer," Ken
muttered under his breath, already envisioning himself
in a total body cast at the local hospital. But then he
thought, *Actually, that's all I do have.*
God, please help me get down this
mountain.

Hear, O LORD, and
be merciful to me; O
LORD, be my help.

Psalm 30:10 NIV

It took Ken three hours to
make his way down the trail—ten
yards at a time, punctuated by fifteen

74

soft-landing falls. A member of the group saw Ken as he took off his ski boots and asked him, "How'd it go?"

"Great morning on the mountain," Ken said, and then added, "I had a three-hour conversation with God."

∽

Prayer is not intended to be a last-resort measure; rather, it is a first-resort conversation with God: an ongoing opportunity to tell him your joys, sorrows, and problems, and to listen for his advice and receive his comfort.

O LORD my God, I called to you for help and you healed me. O LORD, you brought me up from the grave; you spared me from going down into the pit.
Psalm 30:2–3 NIV

God, I'm in a situation that's tough for me. I know I made some mistakes that got me here. Nevertheless, I need your help!
Amen.

PRAYER
Knowing God

God be in my head,
And in my understanding;
God be in my heart,
And in my thinking.

HORAE B. V. MARIAE

God said, "You will seek Me and find Me when you search for Me with all your heart."

Jeremiah 29:13 NASB

GOD IS GREAT, AND THEREFORE HE
WILL BE SOUGHT; HE IS GOOD, AND
THEREFORE HE WILL BE FOUND.

JOHN JAY

 I gave my attention to the Lord God to seek Him by prayer and supplications.

Daniel 9:3 NASB

He has satisfied the thirsty soul,
And the hungry soul He has filled with what is good.

Psalm 107:9 NASB

Knitting with God

Claudia felt that her life was unraveling. She complained to her business partner, Marilyn, "I have too many things to juggle in a day. Yesterday alone I had to leave the office for three separate errand runs and appointments, finish a major project for a client, work out, fix dinner for a house guest, and in the midst, I had several important phone calls at home and at work. I'm feeling frayed around the edges."

Knowing that her friend Claudia was an avid knitter, Marilyn responded, "No time to knit, huh?"

Jesus, perceiving that they were intending to come and take Him by force to make Him king, withdrew again to the mountain by Himself alone.

John 6:15 NASB

"That's it," Claudia said. "I haven't been knitting."

For Claudia, spending fifteen minutes with her needles clicking away on a gift for a friend or garment for herself was a relaxing part of a day. But it was more than that. Knitting time was also Claudia's time to settle her mind, quiet her emotions, and talk to

God. Knitting was what her fingers did while her heart connected with her Creator. She realized for the first time that knitting was a meaningful analogy to her about trusting God to create something beautiful out of her life, one divine stitch at a time.

∞

Meaningful prayer times often have these components: time in quiet solitude, the hands or body doing something that requires minimal focus and rhythmic repetition, and a break from work routines that is refreshing to your emotions and clearing to your mind.

Let the words of my mouth and the meditation of my heart Be acceptable in Your sight, O LORD, my rock and my Redeemer.
Psalm 19:14 NASB

God, please help me to carve out a special time and place each day in which I can communicate more intimately with you. *Amen.*

Jesus had compassion on them, because they were harassed and helpless, like sheep without a shepherd.

Matthew 9:36 NIV

Seeing As God Sees

Joe, a rural innkeeper, had given his city friend Warren an open invitation to retreat to his place some weekend when he wanted peace and quiet. Warren accepted the invitation one January, happy about the possibility he might be snowbound at Joe's inn, with its well-stocked pantry, diverse book collection, electric generator, and large fireplace for atmosphere. To Joe's dismay, the first evening of Warren's visit, a group of drunken tourists came walking along the lane outside the inn, singing at the top of their lungs, shattering the calm silence of the wintry night. Joe went into the library and was about to rail against the revelers when he saw Warren standing by the window and heard him praying, "God, help them get home safely—to a place that's as warm and inviting as Joe's place. Please don't let any of them slip on the icy roadway or be struck by a passing vehicle. Amen."

You, O LORD, are a God merciful and gracious, Slow to anger and abundant in lovingkindness and truth.

Psalm 86:15 NASB

"You're very generous," Joe said

as Warren finished his prayer. Warren smiled and replied, "I no doubt have disturbed the peace of others on countless occasions and been in dangers I didn't recognize. I'm grateful for a compassionate God and compassionate people."

Prayer helps you see others as God sees them—with a heart of compassion and mercy. Prayer also opens your eyes so you see your self as a person with frailties, foibles, and faults—and in need of compassion and mercy.

Their heart was not steadfast toward Him, Nor were they faithful in His covenant. But He, being compassionate, forgave their iniquity and did not destroy them.
Psalm 78:37–38 NASB

God, help me to be as compassionate toward others as you have been toward me.
Amen.

A Change of Heart

Kendra and Marti found themselves in exactly the same situation—recovering from broken hearts. In Kendra's case, a man she had dated for three years had broken off their relationship. In Marti's case, her fiancé had ended their relationship a month before the wedding. Both women concluded that their men had become scared of commitment. They decided the most positive thing they could do would be to meet together once a week to pray for Zane and Larry. They decided to meet at Marti's apartment on Fridays during their lunch hours.

The young women met faithfully for ten weeks. Each week they focused on a different aspect of their beloved one's personal history in relationships, personality, family upbringing, cultural heritage, faith, and so forth. Finally one Friday Kendra said, "I've prayed everything I know to pray. I think it's time to just rest in this and trust God."

*LORD, for what
do I wait? My
hope is in You.*

Psalm 39:7 NASB

82

"You know," Marti responded. "I feel the same way. But I've also been thinking, Kendra, that my heart is different. God may not at all be changing Zane and Larry. We don't know what's happening with them. But God has and is changing us."

Prayer is never a sure-fire way for you to ensure change or repentance in another person. The primary recipient of prayer is often the person who prays. Prayer softens your heart, strengthens your resolve, heals your wounded spirit, and renews your hope.

Jesus said, "Bless those who curse you, pray for those who mistreat you. . . . Treat others the same way you want them to treat you." Luke 6:28, 31 NASB

God, whatever it is that I pray for another person, help me to realize that you desire to do that same work in me. Amen.

Epaphras . . . [is] always laboring earnestly for you in his prayers, that you may stand perfect.

Colossians 4:12 NASB

Deeper Roots

Lisa and Craig had lived in their neighborhood for two years when Lisa said one day, "I don't think we have much of a relationship with our neighbors. I'd like to put down deeper roots here, and I think that means getting to know them better."

Craig asked, "How do we start?"

Lisa offered, "I think we need to start praying for them. And then I think we should invite them to a barbecue."

Craig replied, "Good ideas. But do we know enough to pray?" As they began to discuss their neighbors, they realized they knew quite a bit about them—most worked, one family had teenagers, one couple was elderly, and one woman was an avid gardener. They began to pray for their neighbors to be good parents, to have good health, to enjoy success in their work, and to see fruit from their

We constantly pray for you, that our God may . . . fulfill every good purpose of yours.

2 Thessalonians 1:11 NIV

efforts. By the date of the barbecue, Lisa and Craig felt unexplainably comfortable conversing with their neighbors. They discovered several practical ways in which they might help their neighbors. "You wanted to put down deeper roots," Craig laughingly said after the party. "I just agreed to help Mrs. Williams plant two azalea bushes."

∽

Prayer opens you up to relate to others in positive and helpful ways. When you pray for them, you have a greater empathy and a desire to connect with them.

We pray . . . that you may live a life worthy of the Lord and may please him in every way: bearing fruit in every good work, growing in the knowledge of God.
Colossians 1:10 NIV

God, show me ways in which I might pray more effectively, give more generously, help more willingly, and befriend more openly the people around me.
Amen.

PRAYER
God's Awesome Creativity

I thank you, O Lord, for the pleasures
you have given me through my senses;
for the glory of thunder, for the mystery
of music, the singing of birds and the
laughter of children. I thank you for the
delights of color, the awe of the sunset,
the wild roses in the hedgerows, the
smile of friendship. I thank
you for the sweetness of
flowers and the scent of
hay. Truly, O Lord, the
earth is full of your riches.
Amen.

EDWARD KING

He who forms the mountains,
  creates the wind,
  and reveals his thoughts to man,
he who turns dawn to darkness,
  and treads the high places of the earth—
  the LORD God Almighty is his name.

Amos 4:13 NIV

LOOK THROUGH NATURE UP TO NATURE'S GOD.

ALEXANDER POPE

In the beginning God created the heavens and the earth. . . .
God saw all that he had made, and it was very good.

Genesis 1:1, 31 NIV

Jesus said, "The Son of Man has come to save that which was lost."

Matthew 18:11 NASB

Until You Cry

Diane and Jerry were invited to a dinner party, and among the guests was a man who had been a missionary in South America for forty-five years. "Why did you want to be a missionary?" Jerry asked.

"Well," the man said, "one night a guest preacher came to my church and said he had two challenges for the young people in attendance. I was only twenty at the time, so I figured I qualified as a young person. He went on to say, 'I challenge you every day to read part of the first four books of the New Testament until you read something that applies directly to you. Then get down on your knees and pray for lost souls until you cry.' The reading part was easy—just about everything seemed to hit me right between the eyes. The praying part was more difficult. I found that I needed to read about people in other lands before I felt enough concern to pray for them until I cried. I started with South America. I read about

Paul said, "You know how I lived the whole time I was with you. . . . I served the Lord with great humility and with tears."

Acts 20:18–19 NIV

their land, their people, their history, and their challenges. And the more I learned, the more I prayed and cried, the more I wanted to live with them and help them."

Jerry nodded thoughtfully. *Yes*, he thought. *Pray until you cry.*

As you pray for others, you'll discover that prayer creates in you a greater desire to reach out to others with a loving heart and a helping hand.

Jesus said, "Love each other as I have loved you. Greater love has no one than this, that he lay down his life for his friends."

John 15:12–13 NIV

God, give me a glimpse of how much you love other people and want to bless them. Help me to have a tender, generous heart.
Amen.

The Job

Miriam had taken her job with the corporation as a last resort. She had graduated from college but had been unable to find a job in her specialized field. Knowing she had excellent typing, computing, and telephone skills, she had applied for an executive secretary position and had been hired immediately. Her boss—a senior vice president—had been highly complimentary of her work and had given her several raises in the two years she had worked for him.

Now, a position had been posted in the corporation for a supervisor's job. Miriam believed she was well qualified for the position but felt reluctant to apply for it, fearing her boss would think she was disloyal. Every time she prayed about the situation, however, she felt her spirit responding with just one word, *Ask.* At first, she seemed to hear this word as a very faint impression in her mind, but the more she prayed, the stronger the impression grew. Finally she sum-

Since you are my rock and my fortress, for the sake of your name lead and guide me.

Psalm 31:3 NIV

moned her courage and asked to be considered for the position. She knew that regardless of the outcome, she had been true to her heart's deepest desire.

∽

Three of the ways God answers a prayer for guidance are by giving you a fresh new idea, by giving you an idea repeatedly, and by giving you an idea that stirs you to positive action. The ideas, of course, must be ideas for doing good.

I will instruct you and teach you in the way you should go; I will counsel you and watch over you.
Psalm 32:8 NIV

God, I think I know what I want. If this is right for me, help me to take action. If it's wrong for me, give me a new desire.
Amen.

The LORD said, "Call to me and I will answer you and tell you great and unsearchable things you do not know."

Jeremiah 33:3 NIV

Go When You Know

Harry was stunned by the medical diagnosis he was given and hardly knew how to respond. In some moments, he was panic-stricken. At other times he felt numb. "What shall I do, God?" Harry prayed. "Please show me how to deal with this."

Harry decided he wouldn't tell anyone about his medical problem until he had a game plan for addressing it. He did, however, continue to pray nearly continuously for God to show him what to do. On Sunday, his pastor preached a sermon titled, "There's Hope." On Monday, a friend told Harry over lunch about a former coworker who had just returned from a major medical center—he had been treated for the precise ailment Harry had. Two days later, another friend said out of the blue, "Say, Harry, if you ever need for me to take care of your plants or pets while you're away, just say so. I'll gladly do that for you." The next day, Harry's boss asked if Harry would like to sign up for a

God said, "I am the LORD your God . . . Who leads you in the way you should go."

Isaiah 48:17 NASB

voluntary program to take an extra month's vacation at one-quarter pay but full benefits. David could hardly believe how things were falling into place. All of his concerns were being addressed. Coincidence? Not as far as Harry was concerned.

One of the ways in which God answers your prayers is to give you information and encouragement through the words of other people—often in ways that you don't ask for and don't expect.

O Lord, lead me in Your righteousness because of my foes; Make Your way straight before me.
Psalm 5:8 NASB

God, I sometimes don't know which way to turn. Please show me. I won't go until I know how you want me to proceed.
Amen.

Be considerate . . . so that nothing will hinder your prayers.

1 Peter 3:7 NIV

Clearing the Way

David finally reached "critical motivational mass." He had filled his garage with objects—everything from unused exercise equipment to old business files—to the point he could no longer park his car in it. As a consequence, he had spent dozens of hours in the last year scraping ice from his car in the winter, washing his car after dust storms, and hoping his car wouldn't be damaged by hail. He set aside a Saturday to clean out his garage and found himself muttering, "Why did I let this happen? What a waste of time and energy. I can hardly move—I feel trapped."

Suddenly David realized, *Those are the same things I said last weekend.* David had confessed to several close friends the previous weekend while on a camping trip that he felt locked into a dead-end job, that he had been wasting a lot of time in trivial conversations, and that he had allowed bad habits to fill his time and negative thoughts to

Do not deceive yourselves; no one makes a fool of God. You will reap exactly what you plant.

Galatians 6:7 GNT

fill his mind. "Lord," David prayed, "help me to clear out my soul. Show me what to keep and what to discard so nothing hinders my prayers or my relationship with you."

∽

Meaningless activities and clutter can keep you from developing a closer relationship with God. Thinking about loose ends and dead ends can fill your mind to the degree you fail to pray. Ask God to reveal to you anything—people, activities, or attitudes—that might hinder your spiritual growth.

Happy are those who reject the advice of evil people, who do not follow the example of sinners or join those who have no use for God.

Psalm 1:1 GNT

God, help me to clear out of my life anything that stands in the way of my drawing closer to you.

Amen.

PRAYER
A Heavenly Declaration

Praise our God all you his servants,

Honour him, you who fear God, both great and small.

Heaven and earth praise your glory, O Lord,

All creatures in heaven, on earth and under the earth;

Let us praise and glorify him for ever. Amen.

SAINT FRANCIS OF ASSISI

I will praise you, O Lord, among he nations;
I will sing of you among the peoples.
For great is your love, reaching to the heavens;
your faithfulness reaches to the skies.
Psalm 57:9–10 NIV

THERE IS ABOUT US, IF ONLY WE HAVE EYES TO
SEE, A CREATION OF SUCH SPECTACULAR
PROFUSION, SPENDTHRIFT RICHNESS, AND
ABSURD DETAIL, AS TO MAKE US CATCH OUR
BREATH IN ASTONISHED WONDER.

MICHAEL MAYNE

The heavens are Yours, the earth also is Yours;
The world and all it contains, You have founded them.
Psalm 89:11 NASB

Used by God

While visiting her aunt in a nursing home, Tina was struck by a little placard she saw posted in the nurses' station: "Allow your hands to be an extension of God's everlasting arms."

Tina began to reflect on some of the many ways hands are used: to make a piecrust, caress a furrowed brow, hug a child, knit a scarf, write a note, push a wheelchair, lift a heavy burden, turn pages of a book, and pour a cup of tea. She thought about what it meant to her aunt for Tina to hold her hand as they walked together, and how much her aunt enjoyed Tina's giving her a gentle neck massage or a manicure. She reflected on how her prayer times with her aunt seemed more personal and meaningful if the two of them held hands.

*The eternal God
is a dwelling place,
And underneath are the
everlasting arms.*

Deuteronomy 33:27 NASB

Tina thought, *Our culture tells us we shouldn't allow ourselves to be "used," but that's the exact opposite of what God desires. God wants to* use us to help others. He desires for us to be an extension of his everlasting arms of love, concern, and tender care. She prayed with eagerness, "God, use my hands today."

∽

The sense of touch is linked in the Bible to healing, forgiveness, compassion, and care. When you touch others as you pray with them or for them, you often will find that your hands become an extension of God's loving, helping, caring, uplifting hands.

She stretches out her hands to the distaff, And her hands grasp the spindle. She extends her hand to the poor, And she stretches out her hands to the needy.

Proverbs 31:19–20 NASB

God, use my hands today to do your work. Show me how to reach out to others to help, heal, and encourage.
Amen.

Jesus said, "When you are praying, do not use meaningless repetition."

Matthew 6:7 NASB

Remembering the Reason

Kate laughed aloud after reading this anecdote: A man once felt that his dog distracted him during his morning prayers, so he tied the dog to the bedpost while he prayed. Years later, the man's grandson asked his father, "Dad, why do you tie our dog to the bedpost for a few minutes each morning?" The man couldn't remember. "I think it's for good luck," he told his son. He had forgotten the reason his father had tied up his dog.

Kate began to question some of her own religious practices, asking herself, *Why do I pray? Why do I do the things I do?* She came to the sobering conclusion that she had lost some of her original meaning for prayer and for certain spiritual rituals. *There's something wrong,* she thought, *if I can think about my grocery list while saying a memorized prayer.* "Lord, help me," Kate prayed, "to come to you in prayer with my mind fully on you. Help me to keep

Sing joyfully to the LORD, you righteous. . . . Sing to him a new song.

Psalm 33:1, 3 NIV

my mind free from irrelevant thoughts and to focus on you and you alone. Help me to express myself in new and creative ways, and to be more intentional about what I say and how I listen for you to speak to my heart."

Anything you do by rote repetition can become an empty and hollow habit, including prayer. Reflect periodically on why you pray the way you pray. Try expressing your deepest feelings, thoughts, desires, and hopes to God in a fresh, new way.

I will pray with my spirit, but I will also pray with my mind; I will sing with my spirit, but I will also sing with my mind.

1 Corinthians 14:15 NIV

God, help me always to stay focused on you as I pray. Help me to be creative and direct in my communication with you.

Amen.

Direct me in the path of your commands,
for there I find delight.

Psalm 119:35 NIV

Divine Options

Ned and Carol had lived in their house for twenty years and had seen several families come and go from the house next door. All of their neighbors to date had been quiet and respectful. The new neighbors, however, were different. Ned and Carol found themselves fussing and fuming over the loud music next door, the trash buildup in the neighbor's front yard, and the neighbor's dog that barked unceasingly. They also found themselves questioning the continual traffic of visitors who seemed to come at all times of the day and night. Ned and Carol asked themselves, "Do we call the police? Do we confront our new neighbors? Do we get other neighbors to go with us to confront them?"

"Let's try prayer," Ned finally said.

I said, "O Sovereign LORD, you alone know."

Ezekiel 37:3 NIV

Carol agreed and added, "Let's pray for them to move, or change, or for God to change our hearts, or show us if we need to move."

"That's giving God a lot of

options," Ned suggested.

Carol responded, "I think God likes it that way. We know God wants us to live in peace, but how he gets us to that point may surprise us."

"You're right. And God has more options than we can imagine."

∞

Pray for specific needs, goals, and desires and leave the timing and methods for God's answers up to him. God sometimes changes circumstances, sometimes changes other people, and sometimes changes you.

If you call out for insight and cry aloud for understanding. . . . Then you will understand what is right and just and fair—every good path.
Proverbs 2:3, 9 NIV

God, help me to trust you to answer my prayers in your timing, using your methods, and always for your eternal purposes to be fulfilled.
Amen.

All Day Long

Vera was puzzled by a friend's suggestion that she needed to pray all day long. She asked, "How can I do that and get my work done?"

Her friend replied, "Just pray about every decision, problem, or opportunity that comes your way. Ask God to give you his wisdom and insight."

"Won't God get tired of me?" Vera asked.

Her friend, knowing that Vera was a reporter for the city's daily newspaper, replied, "No, God likes to be interviewed. Pray the questions you learned to ask in journalism school: who, what, when, where, why, and how." Vera agreed to give her friend's advice a try.

Many are asking, "Who can show us any good?" Let the light of your face shine upon us, O Lord.

Psalm 4:6 NIV

The next day Vera found herself praying frequently, "Lord, why is this happening, and why now? What am I failing to see? How should I respond? Who should I call for more information? Where should I go? When should I speak up? Why is this impor-

104

tant to me or my readers?"

She later told her friend, "Thank you for teaching me how to pray all day. I'm not only enjoying prayer more as I ask God questions and get God's answers, but I think I just may be developing into a better journalist."

෨

Prayer is asking God to give you all you need to live a peaceful, joyful, loving, and moral life. Prayer is also listening for God's answers as you read the Bible or reflect on the spiritual message of a song, sermon, or conversation.

As for me, I watch in hope for the LORD, I wait for God my Savior; my God will hear me.
Micah 7:7 NIV

God, I'm bringing all my questions and requests to you today. Help me to listen for your answers and pursue your solutions.
Amen.

PRAYING
for the Needy

O God, graciously comfort and tend all
who are imprisoned, hungry, thirsty,
naked and miserable; also all widows,
orphans, sick and sorrowing. In brief,
give us our daily bread, so that Christ
may abide in us and we in him for ever,
and that with him we may worthily bear
the name of "Christian." Amen.

MARTIN LUTHER

God said, "Do not deny justice to your poor people."

Exodus 23:6 NIV

WHEN WE SERVE THE POOR AND THE SICK, WE
SERVE JESUS. WE MUST NOT FAIL TO HELP OUR
NEIGHBORS, BECAUSE IN THEM WE SERVE JESUS.

SAINT ROSE OF LIMA

*Jesus said, "I tell you the truth, whatever you did for one of
the least of these brothers of mine, you did for me."*

Matthew 25:40 NIV

Direct my footsteps according to your word.
Psalm 119:133 NIV

Without Getting Dizzy

Bored on his daily commute by train into the city, Carl casually picked up a little magazine that had been left behind on the seat next to him. He opened it and read:

"The earth is moving in at least six different ways simultaneously. It is spinning on its axis at the speed of one thousand miles an hour. It is tilting slowly back and forth on its axis to an angle of twenty-three degrees. It is rotating with its moon around the sun at a rate of eighteen and a half miles a second. The sun is also in an orbit, moving at twelve miles a second. The stars are revolving around the Milky Way's center at one hundred and eighty miles a second. And the Milky Way, our galaxy, is also plunging through space at a terrific speed although no scientist knows the precise orbit or destination."

Carl shut the magazine and prayed as he stared out the train window. "And addition to all that movement, I'm going in still another

I have set the LORD continually before me . . . I will not be shaken.

Psalm 16:8 NASB

direction by being on this commuter train. Surely if you can control all that motion without any of us getting dizzy or sick, God, you can direct all my steps today."

Prayer is a way of yielding control to God. It is an expression of trust in God to guide your steps and decisions, protect your life, and provide for your needs without any dizziness that can come from feeling overwhelmed, confused, or lost.

The steps of a man are established by the Lord, And He delights in his way. When he falls, he shall not be hurled headlong; Because the Lord is the One who holds his hand.
Psalm 37:23–24 NASB

God, help me to walk out my day without falling, faltering, or failing. Let me walk without wavering in my faith.
Amen.

Confess your sins to one another and pray for one another, so that you will be healed. The prayer of a good person has a powerful effect.

James 5:16 GNT

Fear, Do Not Enter

Virginia experienced tremendous waves of fear in the aftermath of a bone marrow transplant procedure. Fear kept her awake, trembling, and often drenched with perspiration. She knew this wasn't what God desired for her, and she asked a friend who came to visit, "What should I do?"

The friend suggested she write out three signs. She said, "There's a bulletin board here on the wall at the foot of your bed. Write a simple sign that says BELIEVE and post it there. Underneath it, put a second sign that says NO VISITATION ALLOWED BY THE ENEMY OF MY SOUL. And then prepare a third little sign to be put outside your door. Write, NO FEAR OR DOUBT ALLOWED. Ask the nurse to put it right above the sign that tells us to wash our hands thoroughly before entering."

The father at once cried out, "I do have faith, but not enough. Help me have more!"

Mark 9:24 GNT

Virginia smiled, but later she did as her friend suggested. She asked for paper and a marker, and she prayed as she wrote, "Lord, help me believe.

Keep evil, doubt, and fear out of my room."

That night Virginia slept for seven straight hours, and the next morning her blood count was significantly improved.

∞

Fear can keep you from praying with faith. Fear also can keep you from experiencing hope, feeling positive, being creative, getting well, or being open to new ideas. Ask God to help you pray with more faith and less fear.

Stir up the gift of God. . . . For God hath not given us the spirit of fear; but of power, and of love, and of a sound mind.

2 Timothy 1:6–7 KJV

God, please help me not to give in to fear or doubt today. Help me to believe in you and trust you to help.
Amen.

The Shelter

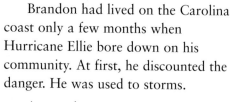

I long to live in your holy tent for-ever. There I find safety in the shadow of your wings.

Psalm 61:4 NIrV

Brandon had lived on the Carolina coast only a few months when Hurricane Ellie bore down on his community. At first, he discounted the danger. He was used to storms.

As weather reporters encouraged residents to seek shelter inland, Brandon hesitated but finally boarded up his home's windows, stocked up on bottled water and batteries, and made sure he had gas.

Then Brandon's aunt phoned from fifty miles inland. "Be wise," she cautioned. "This isn't Kansas. Come up and spend the weekend with me." Brandon told her he'd consider her invitation, but it was only when he saw his neighbors, Carolina natives, loading up their station wagon that he decided he might accept his aunt's offer. "I'm going on vacation," he called cheerfully to his neighbors.

By the time Brandon had packed, he was more than willing to leave. A couple of limbs had been ripped from trees across the street, and the wind and rain had really picked up. "Lord," he prayed as he struggled to open his car door, "I hope I haven't been foolish to wait so long. Please help me."

On impulse, Brandon decided to take the two-lane, slow

112

road out of town instead of the highway. He found the road eerily empty, but at the same time, given the reduced visibility caused by the nearly horizontal rain blowing in sheets across the pavement, he was glad for no traffic. "Help me, Lord."

Brandon spotted a car off the road in a ditch. A young woman was waving frantically to him. Brandon pulled over. "Come with me," he shouted above the wind. She nodded, and with Brandon's help, she opened a car door to get out her daughter and two duffel bags. It was only after mom, daughter, and bags were safely tucked into his vehicle that the woman said, "I'm Kelly. This is my daughter, Meredith."

"I'm six," Meredith piped up.

"I'm Brandon. I'm thirty-one," Brandon replied.

"I've been praying someone would come," Kelly said.

"I've been praying, too," Brandon said as he swerved to miss a large cardboard box.

"God, keep us safe," Kelly said, to which Brandon replied, "Amen, amen."

Brandon mused aloud as they continued down the road, "There's not as much traffic as I thought there'd be." No sooner were the words out of his mouth than Kelly shouted, "Look out," and Brandon simultaneously hit his brakes. He skidded to a stop ten feet from a washed-out bridge. "Thank you, Lord," Kelly said. Brandon again replied, "Amen, amen."

It was only after they stopped that they saw an elderly couple standing beside the road. Their car was nearly hidden from view in nearby brush. Brandon hopped out to help them into his vehicle. "We didn't see the bridge out," the woman shouted above the roar of the storm. "We skidded into the bushes."

"We've been praying," Meredith said as she welcomed the two drenched passengers to the back seat.

"We've been praying, too, honey," the elderly woman replied, shuffling their bags to the back luggage area. "We're Mr. and Mrs. Garrison."

A few miles back up the road, their problems compounded. A second bridge had washed out. As Brandon slowed to a stop he said, "We're trapped between two bridges."

At Kelly's suggestion, they took hands and Brandon prayed, "Lord, you know where we are and what's happening. Please protect us. Give us wisdom to know what to do."

Brandon called 911 on his cell phone and was told help might not arrive for twenty-four hours. The dispatcher advised him to seek high ground should the creeks overflow. Brandon drove about a hundred yards and parked on what seemed to be a rise in the road. "I've got bottled water," Brandon said.

"We have sandwiches," Mrs. Garrison added.

"I have a couple of apples," Kelly said.

Meredith pulled out a candy bar. "I'll share."

As afternoon turned into night, the passengers shared their life stories, including their faith stories about how important

God was in their lives. It seemed each of them had a story of God's provision that built up their faith to believe for a safe night and a speedy rescue. They then adjusted the luggage to create somewhat comfortable sleeping conditions.

Late the next morning, the fury of the storm seemed to pass. About noon, a state emergency vehicle pulled up next to them. The officer said, "We've cleared a path down a country lane to get you to an alternate road. Let's move quickly while we're in the eye of the storm."

"Thank you, Lord," Kelly prayed. "Amen, amen," said Meredith as she looked at the Garrisons and added, "That's what Brandon says." They quickly added, "Amen, amen."

Within an hour, Brandon had dropped off the Garrisons at their daughter's home. He drove Kelly and Meredith to the home of Kelly's friends a couple of miles further inland. They invited Brandon to stay with them, too, and he gratefully accepted.

Two days later, Brandon pulled back into his driveway just as his neighbors were unloading their car. His neighbor called in jest, "How was your vacation?"

"Actually," Brandon replied. "I went on a prayer retreat."

You will always show me the path that leads to life. You will fill me with joy when I am with you. You will give me endless pleasures at your right hand.

Psalm 16:11 NIrV

*Answer me now, LORD!
I have lost all hope.*

Psalm 143:7 GNT

Fret Thee Not

Linda was known by all her friends for having high anxiety. Her grandmother called her a "fretter." For her part, Linda laughed in agreement with her friends and grandmother and readily admitted that she was a worrier by nature. Then Linda began to awaken every night about 3:00 o'clock, and she found that her worrying kept her awake for two or more hours.

Feeling sleep deprived, Linda sought out the counsel of a friend. She said, "I worry about what could happen or what might happen or what seems sure to happen."

Her friend countered, "But you don't know with certainty that these things will happen."

Linda admitted, "No, but how can I break this cycle of worry?"

Jesus said, "Do not worry about tomorrow; for tomorrow will care for itself.

Matthew 6:34 NASB

Her friend suggested, "The one thing you can count on is that God will happen. Pray every time you think of a negative possibility, 'God, if this happens, I'm trusting you will also happen, and that your power, wisdom, and love will turn this problem into a solution.'" To reinforce her advice, Linda's friend then gave her a little cross-stitched, framed statement to sit on her nightstand. It read, FRET THEE NOT, GOD IS A HAPPENING GOD.

Prayer can help you refocus your thinking from what could happen, might happen, or even what will happen to a position of trust that if a problem arises, God will either eliminate the problem or help you get through it.

Do not be anxious about anything, but in everything, by prayer and petition, with thanksgiving, present your requests to God. And the peace of God, which transcends all understanding, will guard your hearts.
Philippians 4:6–7 NIV

God, help me to replace all worry about what might happen with trust that you will be present to handle what does happen.
Amen.

Incline Your ear to me, hear my speech.
Wondrously show Your lovingkindness.

Psalm 17:6–7 NASB

Become What You Pray

Tom had been praying for several days about his strained relationship with his wife, Dena. It seemed to Tom that no matter what he said, Dena found fault with him. He was tired of arguing and was frustrated that he couldn't really nail down what the arguments had been about. As he reflected over his prayers during the previous week, Tom realized that at the outset, he had mostly vented his pain, anger, and frustration in his prayers. Tom smiled as he noted that those prayers seemed to have been answered with a measure of peace and comfort that he hadn't felt before.

Then his prayers had become prayers that asked God to change Dena's attitudes and perspectives. As Tom reflected on those prayers, he concluded somewhat wryly that God seemed to have changed his attitude and perspective instead.

Give me the desire to
obey your laws rather
than to get rich.

Psalm 119:36 GNT

Tom's prayers finally had become ones asking God to help him become a more patient, kind, and understanding husband. Those prayers, Tom

118

decided, were the most important ones. "Lord," Tom prayed, "thank you for hearing me and for doing your work in me."

∽

Prayer creates a climate for divine change, which can include a new attitude, a new perspective, a new demeanor, and new behavior. Rather than ask God to change another person, ask God to mold and make you into the person he desires for you to be.

I directed my mind to know, to investigate and to seek wisdom and an explanation, and to know the evil of folly and the foolishness of madness.
Ecclesiastes 7:25 NASB

God, you know what I need, and who I need to become. Change me in the ways I need to change. Amen.

PRAYER
Bless the Children

We pray for little children, too young to pray for themselves. Amen.

WRITTEN BY YOUNG PEOPLE IN KENYA

Jesus said, "Let the little children come to me, and do not hinder them, for the kingdom of God belongs to such as these."

Mark 10:14 NIV

THE HEART OF A CHILD IS THE MOST PRECIOUS
OF GOD'S CREATION. NEVER BREAK IT.
AT ALL COSTS, NEVER BREAK IT.

JOSEPH L. WHITTEN

Jesus took the children in his arms, put his hands on them and blessed them.

Mark 10:16 NIV

Jesus said, "Everyone who asks receives; he who seeks finds; and to him who knocks, the door will be opened."

Matthew 7:8 NIV

Asking, Knocking, Seeking

While sitting in her dentist's office, Brenda found herself increasingly upset at how long she had been waiting for her appointment. It seemed her entire day had been filled with unproductive rushing and frustrated waiting. She picked up a magazine on the waiting room table and read this poem by an unknown author:

I got up early one morning and rushed right into the day; I had so much to accomplish I didn't have time to pray.

Troubles just tumbled about me and heavier came each task. Why doesn't God help me, I wondered. He answered, You didn't ask.

I tried to come into God's presence, I used all my keys at the lock. God gently and lovingly chided, Why child, you didn't knock.

Seek the LORD while he may be found; call on him while he is near.

Isaiah 55:6 NIV

I wanted to see joy and beauty but the day toiled on gray and bleak. I called on the Lord for the reason. He said, You didn't seek.

122

I woke up early this morning and paused before entering the day. I had so much to accomplish that I had to take time to pray!

"Forgive me, Lord," Brenda prayed, "for not coming to you first so you could organize my day."

∾

Prayer can help you see your life, as well as the lives of those around you, from God's perspective. Prayer can give you new insight into how to organize a schedule, plan an agenda, and define what you really need. It can give you a new perspective on your day.

Hear my voice when I call, O LORD; be merciful to me and answer me. My heart says or you, "Seek his face!" Your face, LORD, I will seek.
Psalm 27:7–8 NIV

God, I ask for your help, your comforting and powerful presence, and your wisdom today. I need you in every minute of my day.
Amen.

It is good to sing praises unto our God;
for it is pleasant; and praise is comely.

Psalm 147:1 KJV

Always the Right Time

Mary and Andrew were sitting quietly and cozily in front of their blazing fireplace one winter's evening when Mary said, "A penny for your thoughts."

Andrew replied, "I've just been thinking about all the things we have to be thankful for."

"Warmth and a soft afghan and the children safely tucked into bed," Mary said.

"A great dinner and a roof over our heads and a job," chimed in Andrew.

"And everyone in our family healthy and the children doing well in school," added Mary.

"And even if we didn't have all these things," Andrew continued, "we have a relationship with God, and he helps us to endure hard times."

Mary added, "And we have church friends to pray with us and comfort us."

To him who sits on the throne . . . be praise and honor and glory and power.

Revelation 5:13 NIV

124

The two sat quietly for a few moments, and then Mary said softly, "We don't praise God enough, do we?"

Andrew replied, "No, and I don't suppose we could ever praise God enough. It would take every minute of every day to praise God for everything worthy of his praise."

Mary responded, "Perhaps that's what eternity is all about."

∞

When you focus on the goodness, generosity, and mercy of God, you are likely to find that it is very easy to praise God. Think about those things that are pure, holy, right, good, and kind—they are all worthy of praise. The list of God's marvelous deeds is virtually endless in your life.

Every good and perfect gift is from above, coming down from the Father of the heavenly lights, who does not change like shifting shadows.

James 1:17 NIV

God, help me to praise you more—in all things, for all blessings, and most of all, solely because you are worthy of praise always.
Amen.

At Inspirio we love to hear from you—your
stories, your feedback,
and your product ideas.
Please send your comments to us
by way of email at
icares@zondervan.com
or to the address below:

Attn: Inspirio Cares
5300 Patterson Avenue SE
Grand Rapids, MI 49530

If you would like further information
about Inspirio and the products we
create please visit us at:
www.inspiriogifts.com

Thank you and God bless!